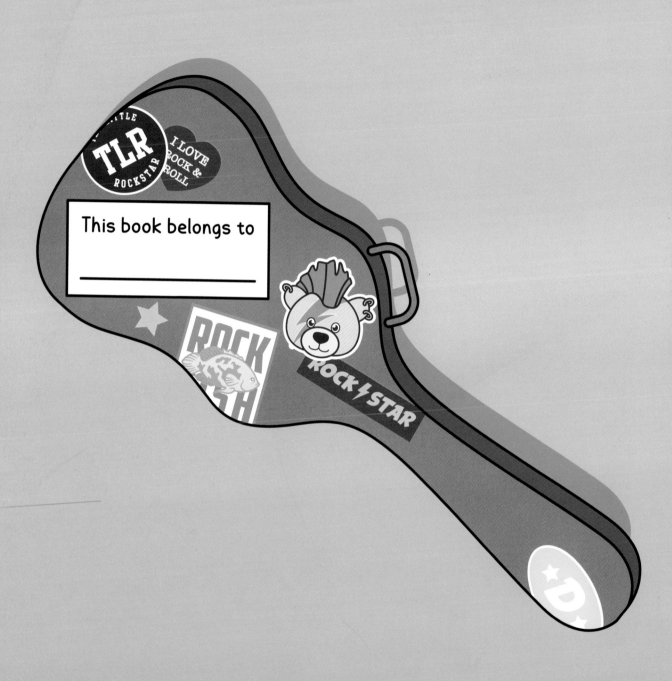

This book belongs to

_____

ABC/DC

Illustrations by Alex Lehours

is for
AC/DC
and they are thunderstruck

is for

The Beatles

and they all live in a yellow submarine

is for

Coldplay

and they wrote a song for you

is for

David Bowie

and he was a hero, just for one day

is for

Elvis

and he ain't nothing but a hound dog, crying
all the time

is for

Foo Fighters

and they are learning to fly

is for

Guns N' Roses

and they want to welcome you to the jungle

is for

Jimi Hendrix

and he has a purple haze all around him

is for

Iggy Pop

and he rides and he rides through
the city's backsides

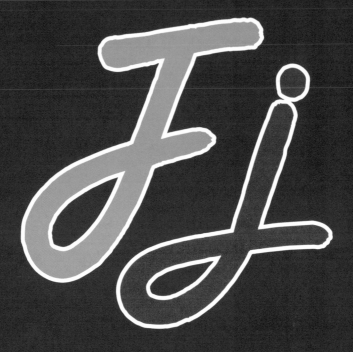

is for

Joan Jett

and she wants to put another dime in the
jukebox, baby

is for

KISS

and they want to rock and roll all night
and party every day

is for

Led Zeppelin

and they come from the land of the ice and snow

Mm

is for

Metallica

and they are the masters of puppets

is for

Nirvana

and they are locked inside a heart-shaped box

is for

Ozzy Osbourne

and he's going off the rails on a crazy train

is for

Pink Floyd

and they're swimming in a fish bowl

is for

Queen

and they've got mud on their face,
kicking their can all over the place

is for

The Rolling Stones

and they are men of wealth and taste

is for

Steve Nicks

and she is just like the white-winged dove

is for

Tina Turner

and she is simply the best, better than all the rest

is for

U2

and they still haven't found what

they're looking for

is for

Van Halen

and they are going to go ahead and jump

is for

The Who

and they are pinball wizards

is for

INXS

and they were standing there when

two worlds collided

is for

Neil Young

and he keeps searching for a heart of gold

is for

ZZ Top

and the girls are crazy about these
sharped dressed men